Dinosaurs' Valentine

I RAWR YOU!

Coloring Book for Kids

This Dino Valentine Book Belongs to

....

....

COLOR TEST PAGE

I
LOVE
YOU
!

I RAWR YOU !

HAPPY
VALENTINE'S DAY

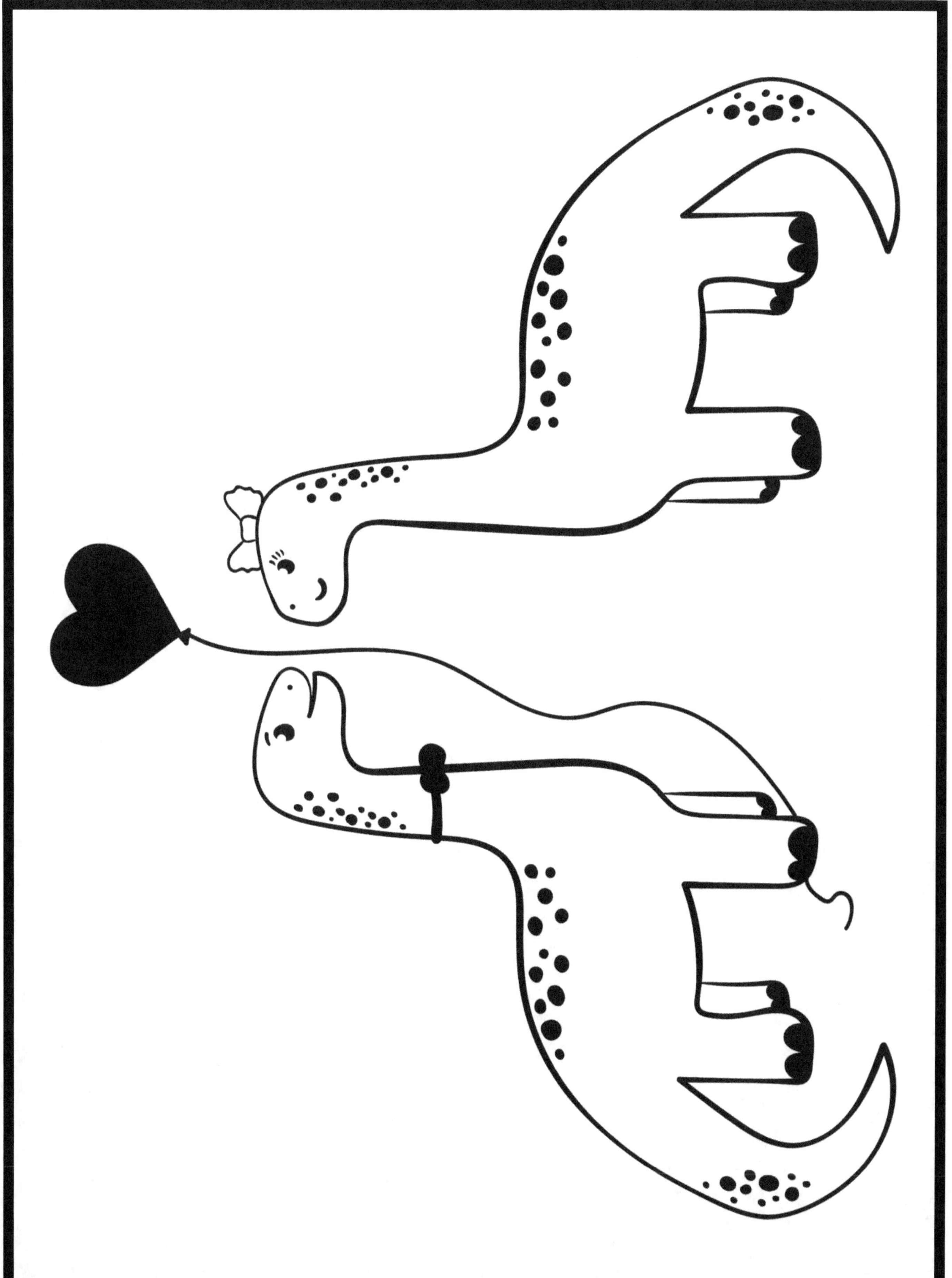

love
bites

HEART
CRUSHER

I STEAL
HEART

You're
MY DINO-MITE

YOU ARE
ROAR-SOME

RAWR
MEANS
"I LOVE YOU"
IN DINOSAURS

LOVESAURUS